All About Feelings

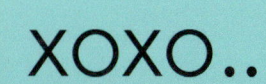

An alphabet book for emerging readers

Written by
Rebecca Eisenberg, MS, CCC-SLP
Certified Speech Language Pathologist

Illustrated by Harry Pixel

Copyright © 2020 by Rebecca Eisenberg

All rights reserved. No part of this book may be used or reproduced by any means, graphic, electronic, or mechanical, including photocopying, recording, taping, or by any information storage retrieval system, without the written permission of the publisher except in the case of brief quotations embodied in critical articles and reviews.

awesome

A is for **awesome**

I feel **awesome** when I am understood.

B is for busy

I am busy when I listen to my teacher.

calm

C is for calm
I feel calm when I listen to music.

dizzy

D is for dizzy
When I spin myself, I feel dizzy.

E is for **excited**

I am **excited** when I play at the park with my friends.

frustrated

F is for **frustrated**

I feel **frustrated** when I can't communicate how I feel.

great

G is for great

I feel great when I eat my favorite food.

hungry

H is for **hungry**

When I am **hungry,** I want to eat.

I is for itchy
I feel itchy when I get bug bites.

jealous

J is for jealous
I am jealous when my friend plays with someone else at recess.

K is for **kind**

My mom is **kind** when she helps me.

lonely

L is for lonely

I feel lonely when I miss my family.

mad

M is for **mad.**
He gets mad when someone takes his toy.
What makes you **mad?**

nervous

N is for **nervous**

I feel **nervous** on my first day of school.

okay

O is okay
I am feeling okay today.
How do you feel?

proud

P is for proud
My teacher is proud of me when I work hard

Q is for quiet

He is quiet when he walks into the library.

ready

R is for **ready**

I feel **ready** to work! Are you ready?

S is for sick
I feel really sick today.

tired

T is for **tired**
When I feel **tired,** I go to sleep.

uncomfortable

U is for **uncomfortable**
I feel **uncomfortable** in this sweater.

victorious

V is for victorious
When I finish my homework,
I feel victorious!

wet

W is for **wet**
When I get out of the pool, I feel **wet.**

XOXO

X is XOXO
I feel love when I type XOXO.

Y is for yucky
The slime feels yucky.

z

zealous

Z is for **zealous**
My parents are **zealous**
in helping me be the best communicator!

Made in United States
Troutdale, OR
10/11/2024

23682261R00019